Joanne S. Duffin is a published author, both as a chapter writer in the book, *Chicken Soup for the Soul: Find Your Inner Strength*, and in the book of poetry written with her son Marcus L. Duffin, *Spilling the Ink of My Soul: A Mother and Son's Journey*. Joanne has been a singer-songwriter for over thirty years. Her most recent album, "Apricot Sunrise," was released in March 2023, followed by a sold-out album release concert. She has been a photographer for twenty years and has won numerous awards for her photography.

To my husband of 47 years, Steven Duffin, my alpha and omega, and my number one fan.

To my four children, Christopher Duffin, Ryan Duffin, Julia Wetherbee, and Marcus Duffin, for giving me the opportunity to be a mom.

To my parents, Doug and Elna Stephenson, who taught me to love learning, and encouraged my talents.

To all the literary giants I've loved over the years, especially the poet, Alfred, Lord Tennyson.

Joanne S. Duffin

WE THE PEOPLE

Poems of Conscience

AUSTIN MACAULEY PUBLISHERS™

LONDON • CAMBRIDGE • NEW YORK • SHARJAH

Ordering Information
Quantity sales: Special discounts are available on quantity purchases by corporations, associations, and others. For details, contact the publisher at the address below.

Publisher's Cataloging-in-Publication data
Duffin, Joanne S.
We the People

ISBN 9798891555570 (Paperback)
ISBN 9798891555587 (Hardback)
ISBN 9798891555600 (ePub e-book)
ISBN 9798891555594 (Audiobook)

Library of Congress Control Number: 2024908845

www.austinmacauley.com/us

First Published 2024
Austin Macauley Publishers LLC
40 Wall Street, 33rd Floor, Suite 3302
New York, NY 10005
USA

mail-usa@austinmacauley.com
+1 (646) 5125767

Thank you to my husband, Steve, who listened, and to my son, Marcus, who lent his extensive computer skills when needed.

Table of Contents

The Lessons of Anza

Today,
My grown children
Are returning,
Returning with
Their children
To a place
A former home
We once knew—
And I, with years
And miles between,
Turn and contemplate
The experiences and
Lessons of that place.

How can one
Retrace steps
Nearly lost
To wind and rain
And find the road
Back to the past—
A road strewn
With jagged rocks
And pits
On the edge
Of a mountain?

Now, I harken back—
Back to another time
When a dream home
And remote living
Were our aspirations—
Until the
Consequential pivot
In our young lives
When metal met granite
Bones and flesh

Were ravaged
And all reality
Was obscured
By the infliction
And suffering
Of a single moment.

I remember
Being consumed
By the cataclysm
Paralyzed by fear
Laid prostrate
By the uncertainty
Of the time
And shocked
By the ignorance
And insensitivity
Of others
To our pain.

In deference
To the moment
We then
Took off our wings
Fled our home
And traveled over
Unyielding granite roads
Beneath threatening skies
To put behind us
Youthful longings
Rife with impractical idealism.

With our family's survival
Paramount,
We offered up
Smudge sticks,
Cleansing our minds
Of shattered hopes
And preparing our hearts
For a more promising future.
In retrospect,

The lessons of Anza
Did become evident
And in years hence,
Self-reliance was
Once again eventually won
Familial love
Was strengthened
Trust in others restored
And faith in a
Compassionate God renewed.

The Love Hotel

This room is familiar
How long have we come here?
Loved here?
Worshipped here?

In all seasons
This hotel has found us,
And we it.

We have sought respite
From the happenings
Of everyday life
Refuge from concrete cities
Their sounds and sights.

Here,
We find union
Oneness
Closeness
Where elsewhere
There is separateness
Loneliness
And singularity.
In this room
Fires blaze
Covers shelter
And bodies discover
The vernacular
Of the heart.

In the quiet recesses
Of this room
There is acceptance
And peace
Though war wages without.

In our hotel by the sea
Senses celebrate
All there is
And ever will be
For here we are one
Here we connect
Here is all there is.

The Prayer

Hot the flames,
Grieved my spirit.
Every news report
More dire
Than the last.

How does a community
Survive cataclysm:
First COVID-19
Then rampaging fire
Both destroyers of hope
And harbingers
Of widespread affliction
And grievous loss.

Come to us now
In the stillest moments
As these wars rage
And human suffering
Is rife.

Come stand beside us
As hearth and home
Are decimated
And tears of the stoic
Finally fall.

The destroyer
Will not win this fight
For tenacious
And strong-willed
Are we!

Together as one
We, too, will wage war!
With our arms locked together
Brother to brother
Sister to sister
We will fight these Goliaths!

Together
May our courage
Wane not
And our faith
Remain steadfast
And unbreakable!

In time
May pain once again
Transform into hope
And suffering into resolve.
Bless all our warriors
Fighting our true fight
That strength
And perseverance
Will win the day.

Bless us to this end.
This is our prayer.

The Siren's Call

Morning breaks
The sea is calm
As waves
Gently stroke
The shore.

A haze covers
The ocean
Smoke from
Fires burning in
The south
Mixed with fog.

Bicyclists skim
The pressed sand
And dogs cavort—
Leaving masters
Far behind.

White geraniums
High outside
My window
Greet the day
With alacrity
In anticipation
Of sun.

As seagulls
Dive and swoop
There is promise
Of kites flying
Taut and high
In the strong
Afternoon winds.

Oh,
To visit
The ocean
To feel
The hypnotic energy
Of the waves
And the cool
Clear sass
Of her summer air.

Oh, to succumb
Year after year
To the siren's call
To come! To see!

I will stay here,
Still,
In the solace
Of this place
Breathe in
The pungent air
And exhale
The magic
Of experiences
Until home caresses
My memories
And draws me
Inland.

The Trishaw Ride

The trishaw carries us
Along a concrete path
Beside the Poudre River
As it winds and bends.

Nearby, green fields caress the ground
And groves of cottonwood trees
Bend and bow to Scrub brushes beneath.

The sky is awash with sparrow blue
And is punctuated by feathery clouds—
The mid-morning sun dancing
Amid the tree tops
As it kisses the blue heron in flight
Swooping over the slow-moving water.

Marsh plants lay huddled
Alongside the river's edge
And grasshoppers cavort beneath
The shadow of the trishaw.

Prairie dogs tentatively surface
From their earthen mounds
To warm their backs against
Sun's morning rays
And the trishaw
With its rhythmic gait—
Though not a quadruped—
Canters like a horse
Along a tree-arched lane.

Oh to be so free
To travel unfettered from earthly cares
And ride in comfort and ease
Through the countryside in Fall
Along the Poudre River!

The Virtuoso's Violin

for Christian Li

Ethereal,
The strings of the violin
Are stroked by the virtuoso.
With his deft skill
The instrument
Powerfully and emotionally
Weeps the strains of
Massenet's "Thaïs-Méditations."

The master is young
But so exquisite
Is his rendition
Of this masterpiece
That the earth on its axis
Pauses for an instant
To embrace the majesty
Of the moment.

The melody
Pure and constant
Rallies for the crescendos
While pianissimos submit to
The changing sounds and intensity
Rising from the calm.

An observer and participant,
I embrace the lilting harmony
As it conveys to my
Open ears and heart
The musical swells then diminuendos
Of a rousing piece of art.

Chills engulf me!
Heart rhythms succumb
To the revolutionary music
And I am undone!
Transfixed in the splendor!

Music!
The gift of the Gods
Realized by geniuses
Performed for the masses
Come to us now
On wings of light
That all may be edified!

The Wisdom of the Seasons

Morning's light
Crests over the house tops
The neighborhood lay sleeping still
As another Sunday dawns.

Spring is here
And soon the tendrils
Of the waking sun
Will cast their rays
Deep into Mother Earth
And summer will be upon us
Once more.

I ponder the knowing
And wisdom of the seasons
That cycle throughout every year
Bringing us diverse weather:

The snows of Winter
The rains of Spring
The sun of Summer
The winds of Fall.
How sure I am
There is a master planner,
One who knowingly orchestrates
All this changing
And becoming!

How grateful I am
That in the dead of winter
There is Spring peeking around the corner
Waiting to burst forth!

How thankful I am
For the colors of Fall that beckon me
From the treetops

And the restless Summer
That plays at my feet!
Oh, to be so blessed
To be always renewing
Always transforming
Ever awakening!
Ever heralding the new day!

Unity

There is a word
In the lexicon of a nation
That, if embraced,
Could propel a people
To greatness
And dispel the need
For war.

It challenges the low bar
Of complacency
Emboldens dreamers
To reach beyond
The confines of daily living
And begs for empathy
Brother to brother.

This word furthers
Noble endeavor
Encourages diversity
Promotes the sharing
Of creative thought.

Without the conscious
Embrace of it
Nations divide
And never conquer
Strife and rage are rife
And wounds fester.

Oh then, Father
Bless this nation—
Our beloved America
And in this our time of need
Guide us all
To the healing waters
Of unity.

For in unity
There can be progress! In unity
There is the bright promise
Of peace!

We Are the Change That We Seek

As I sit alone at home
Contemplating upcoming elections
Never has there been a time
Never has there been such a need
For a change in our Republic!

It's incumbent on all of us
To examine and reexamine
Our hearts and beliefs—
Our commitment
To the ideals of our Constitution
And to our American democracy!

So, I say Rise up!
There is no time to question your
Singular value and importance
In this mighty fight!
No time to cower behind front doors
Or bedroom windows
And fail in your duty to vote!

All Americans who can vote
Must vote to preserve
American life at its best for
"We are the change
That we seek!"

We cannot point to
The right or the left
Presume that another
Take up the cause, no!
"We are the ones
We've been waiting for!"

So, stand up!
Falter not!
Strengthen your resolve!
Be ever-watchful and valiant
For there are those among us
Who seek to destroy
All that is good about America
Sow discord and disharmony
Cultivate hate and foster injustice!

Only you and I have the power
Power in our vote
Power in the collective voice of one
For from this effort
True victory over evil will be won
Freedom over oppression will cease
Progress will happen
Productivity will return
And goodness will be restored!

"Yes, we are the change that we seek!"

(Inspired by Mahatma Gandhi)

We the People

Threads bound together as one
In a "single garment of destiny,"
We the people
Of the United States of America
At this juncture in time
Will share a collective fate:
To retain our freedoms
Or be shackled.

Who we choose to guide us
Out of this country's deepening abyss
Is of utmost import
For the soul of our nation
Hangs precariously
In the balance.

We must, therefore,
Choose those who will lead
By the power of their example,
Not by the example of their power.
Realizing, too,
That no good leader stands alone
But must in humility
Seek a higher strength
Beyond themselves.

We must find those
Who would lead by inclusion
With dignity for all
For no human being
Willing to be a standard-bearer
For freedom and justice
Can or will be illegal!

We the people, then,
Need a builder of bridges
Not an erector of walls
For if a person
Is more fortunate than another,
Let he or she make a longer table
Not build a taller fence.
The gavel of history
Will come down in judgement
On us all at some future time
To ascertain the measured prudence
Of our choices.

It is not too late to change
The current course of America
But the sands in the hourglass
Are precipitously falling
And the moment of decision
Is upon us all.

We the people
Have the power!
We the people
Have the knowledge!
We the people
Hold within our hands
The favored destiny of America!

Remember:
"Change will not come if we wait
For some other person…
For some other time.
We are the ones
We've been waiting for.
We are the change
That we seek."

(Inspired from quotes by Martin Luther King Jr., Joe Biden,
and Barack Obama)

A Good Man

He begins as one of them—
Smug, self-righteous,
Self-aggrandizing, judgmental.

He sees the suffering of others
As penitence for a weak mind—
Their inability to prosper within society
As the evidence of poor breeding,
Inferiority, undesirability.

There is a path he walks
A course he adheres to everyday—
His is a straight, narrow road.
He is self-assured and in his mind,
Unerring.

Yet, one day he deviates
From that path
Falls into rhythm with another's drum
Walks in tandem with the common man!
Conceit and indifference fall away
Like shingles from a blind man's eyes
And, like a miracle,
He no longer seeks to destroy
That which he does not understand—
Those reviled, the heretical.

A book of poetry is proffered him—
He reads the radical rhyme
And is transformed
By its simple appeal
And masterful syntax—
Its pragmatic nature that draws him in.

Suddenly,
In understanding,
He no longer seeks to betray
Deceive or destroy!
His heart has turned to the sun
And radiance and light are his brothers.

He forsakes the haughtiness of yesterday—
Humility becomes his shield!
He now shelters the unwelcome
Feeding with bread and comfort
The weary and downtrodden.

A simple smile has become his lexicon—
Omnipotent and free
It has the ability to transcend
The social chasms
He once created so long ago.

His friends are ordinary people now
He wears the commoner's clothes—
No more uniforms to define and divide!
To communicate
He need only speak from his heart.

Full circle
He is a changed man—
A man recognizable to himself
One he can be proud of!
For he has become
A GOOD MAN!

Dedicated to all good men everywhere!
Inspired by the movie *The Lives of Others*.

Aloud!

The mob spills into
The Capitol rotunda
Intent on destruction
And rampage.

I look on in horror
From the safety of my home
And watch the television
As the chaos ensues.

Desecration of an
American symbol—
The People's House
Is befalling our nation.

Insurrectionists' flags
Wave boisterously in the wind
Messaging hate and retribution
As rioters scale Capitol walls
And push past police barriers
To storm the venerated edifice.

Leaders of our nation
Are guided to safety
Through secret passageways—
But only after vanity
Has trampled democracy
And Congress' voice
Has been silenced!

Oh, America
Where is the cool calm
Of seasoned leadership—
The helmsmen to pilot us
Out of this threatening storm?

Where are the sane voices
That speak courage and faith
In this time of ignorance
And untruths?

Let us at home
Though filled with
Timidity and dismay
Free from chains
Our voices!

Let us rise up from our
Beds of complacency—
As if Lazarus
Say aloud dark fears we harbor
Admit the failures
In which we are complicit
For the very fabric
Of our democracy, in violence
Is being torn asunder!

Therefore, may we
As valiant citizens—
And those leaders aligned
With the values of America—
Advance with banners
Of virtue and truth.

And, with mouths and hearts
Wide open
Let us clarify with dignity
And declare with conviction
Our allegiance to
The very Constitution
From which our freedoms ring
And our peace and tranquility reigns.

Americans!
Come out of this cataclysm's womb
And be reborn
Of a new cloth
For a new day
And in confidence
Speak your truths
ALOUD!

Apricot Sunrise

The first shades of azure
Peek through my blinds
Stealing the blackness
From the night.
Safe within the womb
Of my bed
I search the room
Following the prisms
On the wall.

Outside's an apricot sunrise
Plucked from the night
Arresting silence
With the call of daylight.
And the palette of blue's
Been torched with red
As fiery clouds are fed
By the wind.

I cannot forget
All the mornings we have met
Face to face
Within each other's eyes.
Now you're gone
And I'm to blame
It will never be the same
Reaching for the light
Without your love.

Outside's an apricot sunrise
Plucked from the night
Arresting silence
With the call of daylight.
And the palette of blue's
Been torched with red
As fiery clouds are fed
By the wind.

Oh, this morning's picturesque
And like bookends on a desk
Frames in my day
From dawn to dusk.
Though my loneliness remains
Yet, like colored cellophane
Now I clearly see
Through tinted eyes

Within the apricot sunrise
I've plucked from the night.
Arresting silence,
It calls for daylight!
And the palette of blue's
Been torched with red
As fiery clouds are fed
By the wind…

As the fiery clouds are fed
By the wind.

Atticus

Rising up from a cauldron of racism
His mythical character
Bears the sword of truth
And the shield of justice.

Humble and unassuming
With prowess in the law
He, measured and calm,
Takes on the proverbial giant.

No one else
Is willing to accept
The challenge of systemic bigotry
For fear of social upheaval
Or personal cost.
This David leads
Without compunction or fear
And with a moral compass
As his coat of armor.

"What is a man's crime
Except for the color of his skin."
He argues.
"Prove his guilt,
For I can find none."

A father, a lawyer,
A neighbor, a citizen,
Perhaps considered as ordinary
In his contrived southern hometown,
Yet, he is extraordinary in his resolve
To ascribe to a higher law:
One where truth and justice
Can reign supreme!

If Atticus could speak
Contemporaneously today
What would he say?
Would he find progress on issues
For which he valiantly fought
On the pages of prose?

Oh, to have a champion
Once again for such social ills!
A hero to battle the Goliath
Of racial hatred and bigotry
In order to claim the mighty victory

Love for all mankind!

August Anniversary

Ecola Creek slowly meanders
Down the waterway
To the glistening sea
Like a serpent,
Its quiet stream
Juxtaposed against
The widening ocean
As waves crash wildly
Against the shore.

Children, tentative at first,
Wade into the safety and calm
Of the serpentine water
As its shallows
Cut through sand
On its circuitous journey
To Land's End.

Sea fowl
Can be seen
Flying on currents of air
Catching thermals
To prime fishing spots—
Hunting posts out to sea.

How beautiful to observe
Land and sea unite,
Streams sending their
Watery tendrils
Deep into Earth's sandy bosom
Then ocean waves
Churning and tumbling
With Mother Earth
Like playful lovers.

I watch until the sun
Sinks below the horizon,
And brilliant glittering waves soften
As light dims.

When night falls
Here on the Pacific
I cloister in here with you
And dream.

Autumn

The last trills of birds
Linger in the trees surrounding
The trumpet creepers
On my backyard fence.
The rusty raven high on its post
Remains vigilant and stoic
As warm summer days dissolve
Into cooler temperatures
And green leaves
Begin to evolve
Into the brilliant colors
Of Fall.

Overhead,
Sun-bleached clouds
Dot the cerulean blue sky.
Bushes are given their final trim
Before the dormancy of Winter
And green grass fades to brown.
These are the signs
Autumn is approaching.

Dogs forsake
Their outdoor sunbathing
For fireplaces aglow.
Pillows and blankets
Find their way to
Living room couches
And smudge sticks
Burn and smolder—
Their fragrance dispelling
The sins of the past
In order to consecrate
The future.

This season pleases me so—
The cider's smells seeping through walls
As stews are prepared
And pies are baked.
Parents and children
Turn to hearth and home
Warming hearts and hands
By the flickering flames.

Oh, Autumn!
Spread your colorful wings
To surround me!
Let pumpkins ripen on the vine
And hayrides begin
That this glorious season
May clasp to her bosom
Her golden majesty
And shed her light
Upon the land.

Bright Star

for Margaret

Oh bright star
Shine over me now
For death has been victorious
My true love is no more
And all is dark within.

Not even a sliver of light
Presses against
My windowed eyes
My body
Shivering from the cold
Will never feel
Your warmth
Your caress
Nor will you speak
Your heart again to me
For its mysteries lay still now
Within you.

How do I go on
When sorrow and pain
Become loss—
When my world's axis
No longer turns
And I remain tethered
To what was?

Hear me now love
From deep within
Your earthen tomb—
You will never again hold me—
That hope lays shattered
Before me
And all familiar—

Your voice
Your touch
Your smell
Will be no more.

Bright star
Blackness has overpowered
My once joyous spirit.
Guide me through
This separation
From what once was
But is no longer

That in this,
My greatest moment
Of grief and pain
Your brilliance
Will illuminate
All that I have been
All that I am
And all I ever hope to be
That peace
Will distill upon me
And happiness
Will be restored
To my soul.

Cerebral Blue

Go interior
Where the natural arc of your mind
Ascends into the moon and stars
Of your thoughts.

Where the cadence of the ages
Reverberates in the dense forest
Of cerebral blue
And the glow of creativity is born.

Sharpen the instrument of your mind, then,
Heavy-metaled and fine.
Cast off doubt
The un-doer of confidence
And independent thought.

Soar far into the universe
That last frontier of the mind
Where innovation and exaltation reside.

Open the galaxies of knowledge!
Unlock the mysteries of millennia
And traverse the genius of forefathers
Into the nucleus of human reasoning
And understanding!

Your eternal flame of exploration
And infinite wonderment awaits
As you journey into
Cerebral blue!

Cocooning

I am within this womb
And transforming
I will not be the same
As before
When first we met.

There are mighty changes
Being wrought
Some I do not
Entirely understand
But, yet,
They are inside me
And, so I must acknowledge.

I would welcome you
Into my world
Into this habitat
Of delicate chrysalis
But I can only
Offer myself
After my metamorphosis
When all has been done.
I will dream
Of our meeting
When you can see
My great awakening
And know
The monumental change
That has transpired.

Then,
In perfect union
We will start again
Not as before
But anew,
And our beginning
Fresh and pure
Will offer new life
Once again.

Connection

I know so well
This body of yours
And you, mine.

How many years has my form
Cast a shadow on yours?
How long have your lips
Traced the perimeters of mine?

Through transformative
And, yes, cataclysmic change
We have still maintained
That physical familiarity
That only two people
Long-connected
Know.

And our hands
With their own unique dialect
Have intertwined so often
I daresay
I could find yours
In the dark
There is such magnetism
In the touching.

If I were blind
I could still trace your face
With my mouth
Or fingertips
And conjure your image in my mind
So entrenched in my memory
It is!

So, here we are
Together still
Though aged and worn
Our bodies.
Let us love more freely
Feel passion more deeply
That our connection
May continue to light
The pathways of our hearts.

Courage

The faint of heart
And weak of character
Stand rigid with fear
Cowardly and immovable against
The encroaching threat.

Though the majority
Begs for misguided justice
Only those rallied by courage
And summoned by the
Power of their convictions
Will speak and act.

To be brave in the face of
A threatening mob
Is never easy
The moral fabric of a person
Must be strong and unyielding.

Now then soldiers from
The vestibule of freedom
Unleash your voices
For the fight ahead
When truth will be disputed
And perseverance required.

Valor will be your shield
Words and actions your sword!
Fight with the revolutionary
Words of history
On your side
For dead men watch
And those with breath
Still await your leadership!

Take your shield and sword
And fight on!

Dark Corners

for Joni

I have often hid
In dark corners
Where flame was forgotten
Comfortless
Withdrawn from
The flow of life
You have found me
Sought me out
With candle's glow
Pressed me tenderly
To your breast
And surrounded my soul
With illumination.

How has my life, once lacking
Come to abundance now?
Through your diligent tending
Your unceasing tenderness
Your genuine care—
Else the corners
Where once I lay
Would have forever
Entombed me in darkness.

Dark corners
Still find me
When the silent voice of grief
Overpowers my brilliance
It is then I hear your whisper
Feel your embracing arms
Encompass me with grace
And lead me back into the light.

Encroaching Winter

Crisp air
Breathes in Northern winds and rain.
Leaves twist frantically within
The pale gray sky.

Now Fall is over
And the remnants
Of Her season
Lay sodden upon
The swollen earth
Creating layers of
Brown detritus
That cover walkways
And flower beds.

The skeletal trees
Nearly bare of Fall's leaves
Stand as sentinels to
The encroaching Winter
And their leaves
Covered in frost
Lay in random piles
That litter the gutters.

The air is nearly silent now—
Only the sound of rain
Descending upon
Our rooftops
And errant winds clanging
Against garden plaques
Is audible!

Oh, to see the sun once more!
To walk the forest paths
And fairy lands
In solitude
Birds calling
And owls hooting
Among the ancient pines.

Now,
A new world awaits:
A nourishing
Though barren season
Of drenching rains
Floods and high winds
That soon become
Pelting hail and
Soft snow.

The winter season
In her wisdom
Sees the blessings
She will bestow on Spring—
Sustenance to sustain growth
And provide for Nature's bounty—
And smiles.

Each new season
Inherits the blessings
Of the last.
Open your eyes and hearts
And you, too, will experience
The mysteries of Winter!

Eternity's Flame

The tempest's fury
Has left our world
Entombed in ice.
We look at the
Crystalline scape
Outside these walls
And are grateful for warmth
And safe harbor inside.

How similar is our love—
That despite the
Circumstances without,
Within, our love
Has blessedly remained
Cloistered in the
Fiery warmth of love.

Though storms have
Ravaged our lives
And scarred our tender places
With winds of Fate
Whistling through
The canyons
Of our experience
Yet, we have been steadfast
Long after they have passed.

Then,
Let us love together
And with singular purpose
Cast off all fear and doubt.
Laying aside imperfections
May we through Winter's chill
Find warmth by fire's brilliance
That our lovers' hearts
May remain aglow
With the promise of
Eternity's flame.

Free At Last

for Archie Williams

Out of the pit
That swallowed him
Bruised and tattered
From the harshness
Of a life prison sentence,
Exonerated, he rises.

Born on the wings
Of belated justice
He walks through the iron gates
Of a Hell he did not deserve
Into a world that,
After thirty-seven years,
He does not recognize.

Angola, Louisiana,
The Alcatraz of the South,
Was his imposed home
For nearly four decades,
Incarcerated for a crime
He did not commit.

How does one survive
The horrors of a
Maximum security prison
When one's hands are clean
And heart is pure?

"I was imprisoned,
But I never let my mind
Be imprisoned."
He imparts his truth.

Now he seeks
A new life
Where joy and promise
Are the standard of the day
And sadness is no more,
Where he sees the stars
High in the heavens
And explores the deep bayous
Of his childhood home
For he is finally free, yes,
Free at last!

Full Heart

for Nichole and Cash

Nearly five,
With all the physical attributes
Of any child his age,
Still, this child,
Stunningly insightful and precocious,
Does not resemble
Intellectually and emotionally
The typical child of five.

Today,
Without prompting, and,
Blessed with the visage of an angel,
This child,
Loved and happy,
Looks at his mom and
With sincere delivery announces,
Along with an especially long hug,
"You make me have a full heart."

How does a parent respond?
What should a mother say
To such a proclamation of adoration
Except to hug back tenderly
And weep at the words
So heartfelt and pure.

Blessed is the parent
Whose soul is given
Such loving confirmation!
Such consummate adulation!
Thank you, then, child
For this gift so rare
So unrehearsed and earnest
So spontaneous and affectionate!

I, as your parent,
Promise in return
A life unfettered by want

For you will unequivocally know
As I have today
Love and acceptance always!
From my full heart to yours then
I say, thank you!

Goliaths

Though two generations apart
Yet, you, my grandson,
Through DNA and genes
Resemble me.

So it is
That you bear
Many of my attributes
My talents
My interests
My struggles.

How I hope
To impart to you in love
My life's experiences
My knowledge
My wisdom.

How I long to hold you
When turbulence
Discomfits your heart
And confusion
Confounds your mind—
Tell you it will pass like a storm—
That understanding
Will come in time.

I will be there then
Whispering your name
Reaching for you
In the ever-changing light.
I will stay by your side
When you hold your slingshot
In your righteous hands
And in dignity and victory
Slay your Goliaths!

Goodbye My Friend

for Evan

I am of the age
When old friends
Are leaving this life
Some after years of suffering
Others, when living simply ceases,
Softly in the night
When skies are dark
But filled with stars.

Their light
Passes before my eyes
Like comets in the night sky
Bright and fleeting.

Who really knows
When body and spirit
Will join again?
So, with grieving heart
I turn to reminders of you
Your photographs
A favorite poem
A long-loved song.
Somehow, they comfort me.

Memories are like
Waves of energy
Stored within our brain
But felt in our heart.
How I cling to them now
When fire and stone—
The architects of you
Are now gone.

Know I loved you
Here on this earth
My love for you
Perfect and true.
I will rest in a knowledge
I can confirm—
You were and always will be
Important in my life
But like a flower
Whose bloom has withered
You are gone.

Now, with grateful heart
And through a waterfall of tears
I say with infinite love,
"Goodbye, my friend."

Haven

I know this place so well
My home nestled in a quiet neighborhood
Cloistered on all sides
With tree and shrub.

Here I am safe
Here I feel comforted
By all that is familiar:
Nooks, corners, walls, rooms
All bearing my name
With every placement
Of object, work of art,
Plant, piece of furniture.

I feel love within these walls
A safe harbor in storms
It bears the brunt of the torrent
While I sit content within
Hearing only the pounding rain
On rooftop.

As I rest in the
Peace of my abode
I contemplate those
Around the world
Less fortunate
Who have no shelter
No walls for self-expression
Nor rooms providing comfort and safety.

I vow
In this moment
To cease vanity
Or complacency in my plenty
I will show gratitude
For all I enjoy
For this haven
Is a blessing and my refuge
I am fortunate, indeed!

Hurricane

for Janet and Derek

I watch from the seashore
As the waves begin to churn.
The dark winds of night are upon me
Slow and steady at first
Transforming
With every beat of my heart
Into another terrifying gale of destruction.

I stand inert to the threat!
Unable to move or escape
I hold fast to the tree of reason
Praying with every breath
It will not be uprooted
And I, destroyed.

Where is the calm I was promised?
Where is the day of joy I once knew?
Too many hurricanes
Have fallen upon my shore of late
Their unrelenting waves
Beating hard against my door!
Hope has faded into eternal night.
Now reason has left me.
As I cling to sanity
Though sodden and downhearted
The rock of truth
Offers me succor
Amidst the raging tempest.

Hear the hurricane in all its fury!
Hear my cries
Fearing the dawn
When all will be revealed.
Death surrounds me!

Nighttime envelopes me
With all its mysteries.

I cry out for the faith
Simple and unequivocal
I must marshal.
Yes, I will ride out this storm!
I will endure another night
For life, though often times tragic
Is a worthy gift!
As darkness distills into dawn

I turn to the light
Rising in the east,
The devastation
Evident and complete!
Yet, I have survived!
Take this battered soul
And restore her ravaged home
Not to its original condition
But to its stronger self
For hope will not be denied!

I Am Now

A dream
To write
To express
All within
To those without.

Fears
Invisible
Yet discernible
Linger
In recesses
Undisclosed
But known.

I resolve
To capture
The dream—
A beam of light—
An idea forming.

Oh, God,
Take this
My resolve
And affix it
To a courageous
Heart

That I may
Seek and find
That destiny
Lying beyond
The familiar!

I see
The opportunities
In the distance.

I reach for them
As they march
Toward me,
And cling to
The promise.

Steady
I take
Pen in hand
And establish
Word to paper
Rudimentary
At first
The indelible ink
Forms words
Deep within
The well
Of hope.

The talent
Commands
The sentences
Cohesive
And clear.

Life morphs
In an instant!
Chaff separates
And grain remains.

A poet
A writer
Appear before me
I acknowledge
The transformation
Laud the increase
And bless
The gift
The change wrought!

I am no longer then.
I AM NOW!

I Have Been in Exile

I have been in exile
Far from my ancestral home
No longer living or breathing
The doctrines of my youth.

I have left the island
Moved beyond all imaginings
Been cast off
And become separated
From all I have ever known.

Anguish and uncertainty
Have become my companions
As I've sought a new life
Outside the confines of my past.

Attempts to reengage
With the familiar
Have been contemplated
Yet, so desperate am I
To begin again
All such mental wanderings
Have been handily expunged
Never to consider again.

My journey to a new land
Has been fraught
With internal questions
And surrounded by
The turbulent waters of doubt
But strong and seaworthy
Has been my ship
And the shores of truth
Have beckoned me on.

I have struggled mightily
With new languages
And foreign thought
In search of truth.
To my credit
I am finding the moral self
I seek.

Be with me now, oh Father
As I find my center
That, while I live in exile
The true and everlasting way
Will be my home
And my light!

I'm Glad I Have You

for Steven

When all the world
Is under duress
And death lurks
Behind every door,
When neighbors
Keep their distance
And businesses
Are closed and shuttered,
When illness
Like a marauder
Robs us of
Our hopes and dreams,
I'm glad I have you!

When language
Is no longer spoken,
Streets are empty
And traffic
Nonexistent,
When loved ones
Touch only
Through glass,
Necessities are scarce
And store shelves empty,
When masks and gloves
Are our safety barriers
As danger bleeds
Through surfaces,
I'm glad I have you!

For together
We are shelter.
Together we are safe.
Together we are one.

Innocence

for My Children

How can I keep you safe
Free from the injustices
Of middle earth?
How can I preserve your innocence
Keep it intact
When all around you
Cataclysms happen
And wars rage?

I will keep you in my heart
Wrap you in the pure light
Of my boundless love
Hold you close
When the Santa Anas blow
And the rain pelts and ravages
Our shelter.

I will shore our ramparts
Hide you behind
The firing lines
Of battle.

Yet,
If I shield you,
My children,
From all the suffering
In this world,
How will you learn
To fortify your own shelters
Steel yourselves
When torrents fall
Or arrows fly?

Let us
Walk this treacherous path
Together
Holding tight
With hearts and hands
Exposing the cruelties
And savagery
You will surely see
With compassion as our shield!

Come, then, children
Innocence is reserved for those
Whose eyes are not yet open!
You will see
And know life in time.
But you need not traverse the path
Nor witness it alone
For I am ever near.
Together we will see!
Together we will interpret!
Together we will learn!
For I am LOVE!

Jane's Hope

for Jane Goodall

Far off in Tanzania
Chimpanzees live and roam.
For sixty years
She has shepherded their cause
As a conservationist
Activist
Lecturer.

Her hope lies not
In her efforts alone.
Through compassion
And dogged determination
She has educated the world's youth
And taught them
By word and example
How to protect and preserve the earth
For ALL future life's survival.

"Together we can change the world!
Together we WILL change the world!"
She leads the charge!
Over and under
Around and through
Corporations and governments
She has gently
Yet firmly
Garnered change
For her chimps,
For the environment,
For the world!

A light
Amidst the savagery
And destruction of man
Her powerfully persuasive voice
Cries out in the darkness.
"Come, let's reason together!
No fighting
No arguing
Only cooperation!"

For future generations:
To carry on in her stead
To care, to love, to seek, to do!
That is Jane's hope!

Joining

I hear the early morning calls
Of scavenging seagulls
As they swoop and soar
Looking for prey.

The ocean's waves
Rhythmically pound the shore
Their hypnotic cadence
Reminding one of
Gravitational pull
And nature's cyclic balance
Within the universe.

How comforting to wake
To sea sounds
And your sleeping form
Lying breaths away
On white linen.

How thrilling
To know we have
Shared beds and vistas
Foreign languages and locations
Together now for over forty-four years!

Looking back now
Beyond the young years
Of school and children
When our bodies
Sought each other
In private, secluded places
I marvel at our longing then
Our feverish desire
Our audacity at times
Our fearlessness!

And now,
With the sea sounds
Embracing all we've been
And all we'll ever be
Be with me again
As morning breaks
And sea mist cloaks us
That in beauty and love
We may join once again!

Justice

for Ahmaud Arbery

Dear God,
Arms, hearts, and voices
Have opened Heavenward
In supplication
Pleading for rightful justice
Mankind can by law
Attempt to satisfy.

Even with racial hatred still rife
The seal of time has been broken
And centuries of abuse and discrimination
Are laid bare
Upon the judge's bench.
With clear singularity,
The jurors have today
Abolished an injustice
With guilty verdicts.

The indefensible acts of three
Have been exposed
For the world to see
And the law has judged!
No words of contrition will penetrate
The tomb of the lost.
There will be no exculpation
For the guilty
For jurors and judge
Have rejected their lies.

Palpable is the clanging
Of the bells of justice
As the crowd gathers,
Hands clasped in solidarity
Black, brown, and white!

Voices in this sea of humanity
Swell with unabated joy
Born on the wings
Of righteous indignation!

Today, take now
the innocent to your bosom!
Bless loved ones of the lost
And all whose peace and tranquility
Have been pierced
By the thorn of bigotry.
Restore hope, grace, and purpose
To this, our new day!

Land of Enchantment

As morning breaks
Bright light appears
Through my window pane,
And breathy shadows
Steal inside my room
Slightly swaying
To the gentle wind outside.

Five days
I have resided
In this hacienda
Nestled near
The Sandia Mountains
In this enchanted land.
I have broken bread
With dear friends
Watched as the sun
Has risen in the east
And, as night time has come,
Brilliantly crested
Over the mountains
To the west.
I have seen
Your lakes and rivers,
Your majestic mountains
That rise to greet the earth.
I have worshipped your clouds
That dance in the sky
And offer up exquisite sunrises
And sunsets.

Native American lore
And talent abound here.
I look in awe
At their craft
As I walk Old Town,

And breathe deep
Their history
And love of this land
At cultural centers
And museums.

Peace,
I feel you here
Tranquility,
I breathe you in
Like salt air
At oceanside.
I am awakened
By your beauty
And, with heart wide open,
I embrace you
Land of Enchantment!
New Mexico!

Loss

Loss feels empty
Like an old tin drum
Thin-skinned and hollowed out
Without vibrance
Antiquated and of no use.

At its core is
Loneliness
Apartness
Separation from the whole
A sense of being cast off
Discarded and forsaken.

How does one rise above?
How does one fill the void
For surely
There is loss for us all
At some juncture in our lives.

To move beyond the casualty
Fill the emptiness
Will not be easy
It requires a rumbling
From deep within
A commitment
Firm and clear.

Rise, then
From the depths of desolation!
Hear the voice of hope
From within the bowels of thought
That calls to you
Challenges you
To move
Not to remain stagnant
With grief.

So, today
I will take up the engagement
Stare it down
Face to face
Dare it to oblivion
And replant the loss
Unequivocally
With promise
In tomorrow!

Mother Earth's Rhythm

Fewer star-filled skies—
Now trees and shrubs slowly change
Into their colorful outerwear
Then unabashedly
Shed their rich finery
As it fades and falls.
Now Heaven in sorrow
Over Summer lost
Sends her winds' bluster
Down upon the land—

Mornings, dark still,
Linger as we arise—
Pumpkins ripen
On the vine
Dried cornstalks
Line front porches
And Halloween treats are prepared—
All remind that
Fall's season is upon us.

The halcyon days of Summer
Fade in our memories
Replaced by the aroma of turkey
And apple pies.
The burnished coppers
Boisterous golds
And rich crimsons of Autumn
March into the
Deep greens of Winter
As mankind settles into
Hearth and home—
Staying the course while the
Colder season encroaches.

At Winter's end,
Spring, with her reverence
And brilliance measured,
Will send tendrils of life
Above the ground
Into the trees and bushes
And plants aplenty
Rich with chroma
and vitality.
How blessed
To witness such change
Year after year
Season after season
Observing Mother Earth
Instinctively follow
Her intended rhythm.

Mother

Wherever there's a home
She is there
For she is mother.

What does one know of love
For it can be as elusive
As sun to Winter
As longed for
As food to the hungry?
Fear not
For she is love.

No love is greater
Then a mother's
Nothing's as consequential
Nothing's as elemental
For deep within
Each human heart
There's a need for belonging—
First found within the womb
Then nurtured throughout life
For she is security.

All people
Whatever the age
Seek for commendation
For all they are
And are not.
Mother is always there
For she is acceptance.

By fireplace glow
And gathered 'round
She reads
And shares her knowledge
And experience
For she is wisdom.

In her shines
The everlasting light of God.
She is mother.

My Own Light Eternal

for Morten Lauridsen

Where in the stillness
Is my light,
That drumbeat
Of a distant glimmer
Shining afar off
For my eyes alone
To see?

Where in daybreak
Is that eternal sound,
The ancient reverie
From the shores of truth
That calls to me?

Open all I am
That I may hear
And see
And know
The joy of
Light eternal!
Brush your hand
Across my face
That all my senses
May know you
And understand
Your power
And might
And majesty!

In you
I am not afraid
Of my own light!
Help me seek it
And fear not
Its brilliance.

Bless me with
The curiosity
Of the ages
"To strive,
To seek,
To find,
And not to yield."

That in the stillness
And the seeking
I may find my star
In the brightest galaxy:
My own light eternal.

(Quoted from Alfred, Lord Tennyson's poem, "Ulysses")

Nitpicking

I dropped a stitch
The other day
I lost my place
Along the way
Knit to the left
Then to the right
Something was off
Stitch wasn't right.

I tried to pull it out—
Tried to proceed
But knew my pride
Would not concede
I'd made an error
In my count
I'd have to measure
The amount.

Today I've spoken
Unkind words
Nitpicky ones
That have unfurled
Wicked words
That bruise the soul
Words that linger
Hurt and spoil.

I cannot pick
These stitches out
The damage is done
Now there's no doubt
My words were dishonest
It's me I blame
Now I'm in Hell
For the lies I've framed.

This garment
That I stitch is mine
It speaks my truth
One stitch at a time
I want this cloth
I make to be
Made from truth
And dignity.

Peace

for George Floyd

Peace is a five-letter word
When will it come?
Can it be heard?
He was my brother
He was knelt upon
Is the time for talking
Now gone?

My heart feels sorrow and grief
There's no healing
Time's a thief!
Where is the justice now
When hate is rife?
Is there hope in this land
With so much strife?

The time is here, make no mistake
Beat the drum of truth
Old stigmas break!
Hear me now
Though just a voice of one!
Let's shout from the rooftops
Until the victory's won!

So, peace my brother
Quell your anxious soul
Let's join hands
And take control
To end the polarization
Hate and war
Let's leave our anger
At the door.

Placitas

for Margaret

The sky's blue
Juxtaposed against a field
Of white cotton clouds
Soars overhead
As I sit on
My bedroom's patio
Overlooking backyard
Scrub oak and sage.

The pergola
Under which I sit
Has shadows dancing
On the flagstone
As a light breeze
Passes through.
Spiraling posts
Stand on all corners
Like watchmen
Guarding the palace within.

A peaceful sanctuary.
Serene and calm,
It beckons all who enter.
A realm where reflection
And joyful reunion
Are as one—
Where holy men speak
And love's emotions
Are welcomed!

Bird calls
Coalesce with
The raucous sound
Of dogs at play.

Wildflowers scatter
Among the fruit trees
And the sun's kisses
Consecrate the day.

Oh, Placitas
Within the New Mexico I love,
Spread your golden wings
Around my welcoming arms.
Bless me with your spirit
That as I embrace your beauty
Yet turn to go,
I may keep with me always
The memory of your face!

Prescott

for Paul and Cathleen

Amassed in atmospheric blue
Pressed between earth and sky
Cloud formations expand and ascend
Like kneaded bread rising.

Outside pinion pines and scrub oak
Dance within the landscape
As birds dive then splash in puddles
From last night's rain.

Monsoon season is here
And clashes of lightning
Sever the blackening sky
And warn of impending storm.

Rain falls hard and fast on the baked soil
And thunder disrupts the silence in the valley
Faces now press to windows
And watch as Nature restores herself.

When rainfall disappears, and
Cradled in Earth's womb,
Javelinas begin their unfettered wanderings
As wild turkeys dash behind the overgrowth.

Peace and tranquility reign here
Stress ceases to exist
Worldly cares and concerns dissipate
Like errant rain on dry earth
And, by choice, I am wrapped
In the bosom of silence.

Hot sun, now high overhead
Replaces life-giving rain
And mild humidity blankets the land
As evaporation of water and heat rise.

Oh, to be so renewed!
Oh, to feel the heat of the sun on your back
And the silky smoothness of rain water
As it caressed your bare feet.

Here is Prescott, Arizona
High above the Saguaros
Here, the elevation draws you closer to heaven
Yet, tethers you lovingly to Mother Earth.

Redemption for Cheryl

I have never
Contacted you
Too broken
Too angry
Too ashamed
To reach for
All I am not.

So,
Imperfect and unworthy
I have suffered
The losses alone
Then cursed you
For abandonment.

I never knew you
Through personal
And diligent search
Aloof and unavailable
You always seemed.

So,
Impetuously,
And in blindness
And through
Human failings
I chose not to
Witness you.

I'm calling
To you now
In the darkness
Before the light
Goes out.

I ask you this:
"What if I was never redeemed?"
Then in the stillness
I hear myself reply,
"What if I already was?"

(Quotes from the movie "Wild", based on Cheryl Strayed's book of the same title)

Remember

for Elna Stephenson

This morning when I awoke
You had peacefully passed
Into light eternal.

Sadness engulfed me
Until the memories came
And washed away my grief.

There on my Wall of Time
They will remain—
The memories
From a lifetime of living
Now, ever clear in my mind.

You have always been with me
From womb's darkness and
Throughout life's light.
You have taught me love
Through your sacrifices
That came from
The wellspring of
Your selfless heart.

Now as fireplace glows
Your face appears before me
And I am remembering
A familiar scene—
A book in hand—
A thirsty mind.
At your feet
I learned to seek
Knowledge and truth.

How many times did I see you
Hands deep in the work
Of our home
Administering to our needs
Long into the night—
A cook, a seamstress,
A chauffeur, a nurse,
A mother.

How does a child witness
Such familial devotion
And not feel gratitude
For all Her gifts bestowed.

You will be missed
For as your belongings
Are tenderly put away
All our shared recollections
Will linger with me
In my heart.
Forever I can be with you
In my thoughts
See your face
In my mind
And feel your embrace
Warm upon my skin—
And remember.

Sentinels of the Grasses

This Spring
The lupines are
Especially profuse
As I traverse
The Tonquin Trail.

Like sentinels of the grasses
They rise up
In their stately
Purples, blues, and pinks.

Today,
I spied several stands of them
Rising from the green,
Rich-hued and regal.

They have dressed
In their finest attire:
Costumes of brilliance
Afforded royalty.

Tall and statuesque
They remain,
Unaffected by
The relentless rains
And thawing sun of Spring.

Their faces,
Pressed against
The warming breeze
Smile resolutely in welcome
At passers-by.

How loved are the lupines
Native to these
Northwest meadows,
For they remind us
Cold weather is over
And the heat of summer
Will soon be upon us.

When Winter's fury rages
How I long to see
These messengers
Of glad tidings
Heralding to all
The blessings
Of a waking world.

Sheltering

for My Grandchildren

I once found a small bird's nest
Hidden within the arc
Of my outdoor wreath.
I watched spellbound
As chickadees tended to it
Then laid tiny white speckled eggs
Four of them
That, over time,
Hatched and became baby birds.

I watched
With rapt attention
As the hatchlings matured
Then, one day flew away.

That nesting
So reminds me of you
My grandchildren
And sheltering in,
For each of you
Continue to grow
The truth of which
I can only observe
From a safe distance away.

I cannot touch you
For that could be unsafe
For Grandpa, now
So, I watch you from afar
Chat on FaceTime
See photos of you on my iPhone
But it is not enough to satisfy,
This sheltering.

One day soon
This "shelter in place" order
Will be lifted
And we can resume
Our normal interactions.
I hope it's soon
Before you,
Like the hatchlings,
Leave your nest
And fly away!

Soliloquy

I am alone now
My thoughts within
So like rain clouds
That hover overhead
Threatening a downpour
Yet remain aloof.

Still, at times
When no one is watching
The heavens open and
I speak in rivers of words
That cascade down my tongue.
It matters not who hears
For the thoughts spoken
Are mine alone
Expressed to
An audience of one.

My inner voice,
Loud and strident
Speaks my heart
Plucks the strings
Of thought and reason
So often
It is my perpetual friend.

This reverie,
Often repeated
Reiterates songs of love
Wars within
Eternal questions long held
In the bosom of myself.

I do not seek
The sound of reply
From another.
I do not need accolades.
I seek only for confirmation
From my inner self.

So,
Hear me now self!
Listen to my soliloquy
That echoes in the
Recesses of my heart
And is uttered clearly
For it speaks to me.

Speak!

for Christie

When the world outside is fearsome
And I hold tension in
Like a giant band of rubber,
When all within me
Wishes to shout out loud
And release my fears
Dare I speak?
Dare I voice my vexations
Or remain silent
As energy and upset
Build inside?

Is the utterance
Of my thoughts
The sharing of my voice
Tantamount to
Casting pearls before swine?
Should I care?
Does it matter?

I will speak then my truth!
Shout it from the rooftops
Prudence be damned
This is my world, too!
Pronouncements of imminent war
From the pulpits of government
Affect me
Tie me to an unequivocal reality
I did not choose!
Then speak!
Use my voice in dissent!

To remain silent
When all around me there are
Acts of cruelty and injustice
Should shake my conscience
From its proverbial tree!
Move me, then beyond my thoughts
To words swift and clear
Words of verity and condemnation
To move the mountains of change.

Open, then
The floodgates of my heart!
Let my perfect voice ring out
And speak!

Starlight

Starlight watches over me
While I sleep at night.
It caresses all my dreaming
Vision's breathless light.
Waits 'til morning's sunrise
To steal into the sky
It bids farewell to darkness
And disappears as day rolls by.

Nighttime is the silent memory
Of a daylight dream.
Stars reflect the passing moments
Brilliant white they gleam!
Come to me as night falls
Swiftly o'er the earth
There we'll wait in luminous glow
For our beginning
Life's prescient birth.

Ancient mariners have sought
To follow your starlight
Then, too have I reached for you
In the blackness of the night.
Like a million candles lit
You shine for all to see
So, too, do I touched by your light
Seek a higher dream!

Starlight watches over me
While I sleep at night.
It caresses all my dreaming
Vision's breathless light,
Starlight!

Stella

I have known you since birth
Sought you
In the quiet places in your heart
Brilliant white is your light
Clear and bright
In the morning sky!

How I have loved you
Watched as tiny hands grew
Eyes became intense
With curiosity and wonder
Face aglow
With happiness and hope.

Beauty is your natural birthright
Kindness and compassion
Your inherent talents
Leadership, your gift.

You in all your splendor
Are forever enough!
All your offerings worthy
Of adoration and praise.
You are an eternal star
In my galaxy—
The manifestation of love.

I will reach for you always
In the recesses
Of my life's experience
You are my granddaughter
My priceless child of light!
Shine on!

Sunrise

Pink paint
Strikes the canvas
Splashes across the surface
Of the scene—
The ocean scape
Standing resolute
Against encroaching sunrise.

A slight breeze riffles
Through striations of colored light
As waves crash on shore beneath.
Haystack Rock stands
As a sentinel imbedded deep
Within the sandy tide
And the shadows of night
Have long since dissipated.

Seabirds rise against
The currents of air
That travel over the ocean
Spreading their silvery wings
In welcome to the dawning.
All is peaceful and calm
As I lean into this glorious day
Filled with promises
And potentialities—
For today
It is my birthday
And I celebrate it now
When night relinquishes to day
At the ocean's edge
Here at Cannon Beach.

The Abundance of Nature

The lupines are dying,
Their tall statuesque stalks
And plentiful blossoms
Drying and fading
In the late Spring sun.

The meadow grasses
Tall and slender
In all their profusion
Are swaying
To the mild morning breeze.

Oh how I love
My walks in the preserve
When all is silent
Except for the breathless jogger
Or passing bicyclist.

It is then
My active mind is quieted
And I take in
The sense and wonder
Of this place.

The gently wafting wind
Caresses my face
As eyes are wide open
And skin responds
To the warm sensations
Of coming Summer.

It matters not
My age
For youthful stirrings
Touch my heart
With joyful imaginings.

So, I will revel
In the abundance of nature
And all she offers,
For the season of plenty is upon us
As summer beckons in warm invitation
On the wings of spring!

The Battalion

Early the battalion rises
Readying themselves
For the conflict ahead.

They do not know
The enemy that awaits them.
This foe is cunning
Dangerous and swift
Even the most prepared
Could fall victim to its evil.

So, with noble intent
And a shield of compassion
The warriors wage war
Though dressed
In insufficient armor.

Wielding instruments
Of knowledge
And determination,
And with skill and precision,
These frontline soldiers
Push forward
Against the elusive
And unrelenting foe.

Who will be victorious
In the end?
Only God knows
For staggeringly grievous
Are the numbers of the fallen.

Though casualties continue,
Yet, at dawn's light
The battalion will rise again
And with brave hearts
And intrepid spirits
Prepare for battle
Yet another day!

The Columbia River Gorge

The gorge walls
Are tethered
To the earth
Heavy and majestic
Surrounding
On all sides
The mighty
Columbia River.

Green trees
Hug the cliffs
In tufts of green
Appearing more like
Errant sheep
That have spent
Too long
Eating grass
In the meadow.

Birds reverently fly
On the currents
Of restless thermals
Then swoop and dive
For migratory salmon
On their way
To spawning grounds.

Swaths of flat green earth
Are scattered up the walls
Of the monoliths
Looking from afar
Like well-manicured
Golf greens.

The blueness
Of this Spring sky
Is reflected
In the calm waters
Of the Columbia
With the occasional splash
Of a playful fish.
This ancient scene
Known to man
For generations
Still thrills
Still renders one
Awestruck
Once again
By its loftiness
And majesty.

The Columbia River

The deep blue expanse
Of the vast Columbia River
Stretches before me
Calm and flowing
With ancient walls
Of monolithic stone
Lining her banks.

The river glistens
In the morning sun
As rays of light
Caress her surfaces
Illuminating river prey
For circling birds—
Eagles, hawks
As well as shore birds.

Boaters
And windsurfers
Abound here
Especially during
April through August—
The temperate season
When weather conditions
Are ripe for fearless
And avid adventurers.

Oh then,
Look at her beauty
Feel her alacrity
On late spring
And summer days
When sun is high
In the atmosphere
And the warm wind
Unites earth and sky
East and west.

See how her luxurious arms
Reach out to hold you
In all her magnificence
For she is now
And will always be
The Northwest's
Premier river
Of dreams.

The Dawn

The dawn
Has awakened
From her deep sleep.
She arises from
Her night nest
Among the stars
Kisses the dewdrops
Of morning
And yawns
Forgiving
The brutish nightmares
Of the dark night.

Her past is light years
From her now
And her restless spirit,
Longing to find purpose
Once again,
Reaches for
The tendrils of light
Exploding now
Upon her face of gold.
This calm
Clear morning
Offers her peace
And tranquility
To ponder,
To imagine,
To dream!

She wishes for
New beginnings
Where hope drifts
On currents of air
And reason's horizon
Expands and stretches
Beyond infinity.

Oh divine giver of life
Encircle her now
With love
And compassion.

In response,
Hands outstretched
In gratitude and with
Endless possibilities
She seizes all there is
And presses it to her bosom—
And with joy and light
Embraces all
That can be.

The Deepest Part of Loneliness

The deepest part of loneliness
Is when your vocal chords
Catch in your throat
And you cannot speak
What your heart knows.

When silence
Cannot acknowledge
The guttural screams
So loud in your head
Yet so soft on your tongue.

The deepest part of loneliness
Physically hurts!
It is a wound so large
No bandage can cover it.

When one soul
So robust at once
Becomes slight and withdrawn
At next glance.
The deepest part of loneliness
Is when life and light goes out
And sorrow rules the day
When hollowed out and censured
Replaces smiles
And happiness.

The deepest part of loneliness
When wrapped in the bosom
Of uncertainty and possibility
Is the cold hard thought
Of losing you.

The Empty Nest

for Lee

This empty nest has laid
Plump and full of life
Season after season
For as long as my heart
Remembers.

But, now,
The heartbeat of another era
Has upended our nest
And emptied it of its fullness.

Oh, to be ripe
With youth and family!
Oh, to be fleshed out
With cushioned feathers,
Twigs, and vine yet again!

But this,
Our family's abode
High within the trees
No longer serves us:
Our fledglings
Have flown the nest
And all is quiet
Peaceful and calm
On branches high.

How do we adapt?
Move on?
Traverse new terrain
Of heart and body?
Look to a new day
Of becoming?

We, then,
Must fly the nest, too
In search of ourselves
The new idea
The new thought
The other self
The new bird!

Then return
From time to time
Fluff feathers and material
Anticipating our reunion
For families grow
They do not diminish.

So, as dawn breaks
Our nest will lay ready
And waiting
As the ancient call
Of new generations
Turns you
Homeward!

The Gift of Fatherhood

Children come to us
From God
Gifts at birth
Our charges throughout
Their mortal lives.

We grow together.
We impart our wisdom
Our truth
Our love.
They, in turn
With hearts
Wide open and yielding
Proffer love
And unwavering trust.

How we play our role
As Father
Hero
Champion
Is up to us.

But rewards are great
For we become
As they become
We move forward
Into the unknown
Uncharted waters
Of fatherhood
With only our love
And life experiences
As our guide.

We are gifted,
In return,
With a new life
Evolving,
Watching
The tiniest of changes
Developing into
Lifetime character traits,
And we are witness
To these monumental
Happenings.

Like a chrysalis,
Our children
Are transforming
Into themselves.
Our opportunity
To contribute
To their transitions,
Boundless!

Oh, then, fathers!
Take these tiny lights
Which at birth
Shown only dimly
And guide them
Through the rocky shoals
Of life.
Walk with your
Children
Until their own light's
Brilliance
Is evidenced!

The Keeper of My Unspoken Words

for Kate

We have been dearest friends
For over four decades—
Nearly too many years to count.
We have shared secrets so private
Only God has been privy
To the words.

When you've cried
I've felt your tears
Wet upon my cheeks
As though my own rain
For I have resided in your heart
And you, mine.

When I have quivered in anguish
It's been your arms that have
Embraced me tenderly
To assuage my fears
And silence my pain.
When no one else
Understood all of me
And the abandonment of hope
Swelled my river of despair
You, alone found me
And welcomed my silence
For you were the keeper
Of my unspoken words.

Oh how blessed
Has been our relationship
How full our lives have been
As we've witnessed life together.
Thank you for taking

The sum of that life
And cherishing all of it.
Thank you for filling the spaces
Where only emptiness resided.
Thank you for your mirth
That put my troubles in perspective
And returned my spirit
Back into the light.

When daylight fades
On this life
It is your face I will see
When pain and fears collide
And peace fills all empty places
It is then I will wait
For your effervescent glow to,
In farewell,
Guide me home.